George L. Farnham

The Sentence Method of Teaching Reading, Writing, and Spelling

A Manual for Teachers. Second Edition

George L. Farnham

The Sentence Method of Teaching Reading, Writing, and Spelling
A Manual for Teachers. Second Edition

ISBN/EAN: 9783337165512

Printed in Europe, USA, Canada, Australia, Japan

Cover: Foto ©Paul-Georg Meister /pixelio.de

More available books at **www.hansebooks.com**

THE

SENTENCE METHOD

OF TEACHING

READING, WRITING, AND SPELLING.

A MANUAL FOR TEACHERS,

—BY—

GEORGE L. FARNHAM, M. A.,

PRINCIPAL STATE NORMAL SCHOOL, PERU, NEB.

SECOND EDITION.

SYRACUSE, N. Y.:
C. W. BARDEEN, PUBLISHER,
1887.

PREFACE.

In his experience as teacher and superintendent of schools, it became evident to the author, many years ago, that there was something fundamentally wrong in the ordinary methods of teaching reading, writing and spelling. Viewed from the standpoint of economy, the result bore no just ratio to the time and effort devoted to these branches; and viewed from the stand-point of education, the first years of instruction seemed imperfect and unsatisfactory. This conviction, which he shared with many teachers throughout the country, led to examination and experiment.

In 1858, the phonetic system was introduced into the schools of Syracuse, N. Y., and for a time it was thought that the true method of teaching children to read had been discovered. After a trial of five years, however, it was seen that while pupils learned to read by this method in much less time than usual, and attained a high state of excellence in articulation, their reading was nearly as mechanical as before, and few of them became good spellers. The two systems of analysis, phonic and graphic, had so little in common that permanent confusion was produced in the mind.

The word method, next tried, was much more productive of good results than any that had preceded it; yet by this method words were treated as units, independent of sentences, and reading almost of necessity became a series of independent pronunciations, perpetuating the mechanical results of the old methods.

These experiments and their result led to further investigation, especially in the line of psychology. From a close observation of the action of the mind, and of the relations of language to thought, it was seen that the unit of thinking is a thought, and therefore that the unit of expression is a sentence. The obvious deduction was, that the sentence ought to be made the basis of reading.

In 1870 a series of experiments was instituted in the schools of Binghamton, N. Y., to subject this theory to a practical test. The results far exceeded expectation in the direct teaching of reading, spelling and writing; and led to other results in awakening mind and in influencing conduct which were unexpected and gratifying. It is safe to assume that the problem how to teach these branches successfully has been solved.

This little manual is substantially a record of the plans adopted, and of the principles involved in these experiments at Binghamton. It is published with the hope that it may prove a help to those who have no time or opportunity for original experiment, and an incentive to further investigation in this direction.

The author hereby expresses his obligations to his friend James Johonnot, for valuable assistance in the final preparation of this work. The large experience of this gentleman as an educator, and his sound judgment in all matters of education, were constantly laid under contribution when this problem was worked out.

Council Bluffs, Iowa, January 1, 1881.

INTRODUCTION.

Goethe says, "Let no man think he can conquer the errors of his youth." If he has grown up in enviable freedom, surrounded by beautiful and worthy objects; if his masters have taught him what he first ought to know for more easily comprehending what follows; if his first operations have been so guided that, without altering his habits, he can more easily accomplish what is excellent in the future; then such a one will lead a purer, a more perfect and happier life than another man who has wasted his youth in opposition and error."

This statement is an admirable summary of our most advanced ideas concerning education. In our educational processes we have but to ascertain the manner and order in the use of intellectual faculties and power in performing real life work, and then · guide and direct the study of the youth, that they may acquire the use of their powers in the same manner and order.

Some years since, while engaged in a business that brought me in contact with large numbers of literary, business and professional men, I instituted a series of inquiries in regard to their habits of reading, writing and spelling. From the answers received several items of interest were evolved.

First, Spelling. My question was "When in doubt in regard to the spelling of a word, how do you assure yourself?" The answer, in substance, was, "I write the word, and when it looks right, I assume it is correct." Upon further questioning, they were unanimous in the statement that they had adopted this method as a necessity after they had left school and entered upon the active duties of life. Only three or four, out of some hundreds questioned, thought of the word as they had learned it from the spelling book, and these were teachers.

Second, Reading. In regard to reading I found that most of those who had learned to read in school were slow readers, pronouncing the word mentally, if not aloud. Many found it difficult to take in the author's meaning without pronouncing the words audibly. On the other hand, those who had learned to read at an early period before attending school, and many of whom could not remember the time they could not read, were rapid readers. Their eye would pass over the page with little or no consciousness of the words, and they would take in the thought of the author much more rapidly than if the words were pronounced. These persons had acquired the art of

reading without conscious effort on their part or on
the part of others. Such persons could always spell,
and they were able to detect a misspelled word in the
most rapid reading. They also were usually fluent
writers.

Third, Penmanship. The results of observation
and inquiry in regard to penmanship were equally interesting. Persons who do much of original composition are seldom good penmen. I have never found
a person who composed in the hand taught and practised in school. Most who practised some one of the
conventional systems for years in schools, abandoned
it when called upon to perform real work, only to acquire a hand ugly in appearance, and difficult to
decipher.

The conclusions drawn from these facts are :—

First. That the methods in spelling and penmanship, upon which so much time and labor have
been bestowed in the school, are laid aside the moment
the student enters upon the active duties of life ; and
that for the performance of these duties he is obliged
to form new habits under the most unfavorable circumstances.

Second. There is sufficient uniformity in the methods practised in after life, and adopted without instruction, to warrant the assumption that they are

best adapted to real work, and therefore should receive attention from educators.

Third. That in reading, the work of the school, with all its rules and systems, is immeasurably inferior in results to the unsystemized and incidental work of the home.

Fourth. That where habits have been established by school drill they often prove hinderances rather than helps, and ever after there is vain endeavor to escape from their thraldom.

It is in view of these facts, more or less distinctly recognized, that experiments are being extensively made to bring our schools more into harmony with the real activities of mature years, to give to the pupil not only the tools of knowledge, but the mastering of the use of these tools in the discovery of knowledge and its application to human purposes, precisely as he must do in any vocation to which he may apply himself.

The design of this manual is to aid in this work. It is hoped it may prove a help to many teachers who have long been conscious of the defects of the old systems, but have not had time or opportunity to work out a method satisfactory to themselves. The methods here presented are not merely theoretical. They were elaborated after careful study and then subjected to experiment and correction, and as here given they are such as have survived the ordeal and have borne abundant fruit.

It is believed that parents will find here a simple process of teaching reading, writing and composition to their children which will cause little interruption of their daily duties. Indeed the well regulated home is without doubt the best primary school.

THE SENTENCE METHOD

OF TEACHING

Reading, Writing and Spelling.

CHAPTER I.

First Principles.

Definition. Reading consists:—first, in gaining the thoughts of an author from written or printed language:—second, in giving oral expression to these thoughts in the language of the author, so that the same thoughts are conveyed to the hearer.

It is important that this two-fold function of reading should be fully recognized. The first, or silent reading, is the fundamental process. It is often called "reading to one's self," a phrase significant as indicating a wrong conception of the true end to be accomplished. The second, oral reading, or "reading aloud," is entirely subordinate to silent reading. While oral expression is subject to laws of its own, its excellence depends upon the success of the reader in comprehending the thought of the author. The importance of these distinctions is so great that I will consider them in detail.

Silent, or Eye Reading. It is scarcely possible to exaggerate the importance of correct "eye reading;"—of the ability to look over the written or printed page, and, with the least possible consciousness of the words used, fully to comprehend the thoughts expressed.

A common process is indicated by the expression, "reading to one's self." This means the translation of written into oral language. The reader either pronounces each word so that he can actually hear it, or he thinks of the pronunciation. In either case the thought is not formed in his mind directly through the written language, but indirectly after the written words have been changed into oral expression. This process is slow and laborious, it becomes painful when long continued ; and its practice will account for the antipathy which so many persons have to reading books and articles of considerable length.

The object in teaching should be to make every pupil an eye reader,—to give him the ability to look directly through the written expression to the meaning, or to detect at once the unknown elements that prevent the accomplishment of this object.

A New Use of the Eye. The ordinary function of the eye is to take in the visible characteristics of objects.

This is the use to which all children have become accustomed, and they form judgments in accordance with perfect confidence. No child doubts his ability to distinguish his friends, his toys, or any object to which he may direct his attention. Through this sense, aided by touch, he comes into possession of most of his knowledge of the external world. The knowledge so obtained is direct and tangible.

With hearing it is different. While the ear recognizes sound as sound, it has been accustomed from the earliest period to recognize thought through the sound of oral language, until the thought becomes primary in one's consciousness, and the sound of language secondary. Indeed, language becomes so purely representative of thought, that, as sound, it scarcely appeals to consciousness. The child associates speech with thoughts divined from his experience, and never regards it as having a separate existence. The words he hears quicken thought into conscious activity, and he in turn is impelled to express his thought by the use of words.

The child has come into possession of his powers, both of thought and of expression, by a gradual and unconscious process. He has simply been shaped by his surroundings. By association with those who talk, he has acquired the power of understanding speech and of speaking. The kind of speech which

he hears, whether perfect or imperfect, he reproduces.

This fact should be distinctly understood and real-
ized. The powers of speech and of understanding
what is said, both come to the child by a process so
simple and natural that he is conscious of no effort to
acquire them. Speech, objectively considered, is
only a combination of sounds uttered in quick suc-
cession, having not the slightest resemblance to the
thoughts represented; but by the child it is understood with exactness and uttered with precision. The
whole complicated process is matured without effort,
and without the intervention of teachers.

To make the eye perform the office of the ear, and
the hand that of the organs of voice, is the problem
that presents itself in attempting to teach a child to
read and to write. The vital point is so to change
the function of the eye that it will look upon written
or printed characters, not as objects to be recognized
for their own sake, but as directly calling into conscious being past experiences, and so becoming representative of thought. All the efforts of the teacher
should be directed to this end.

At this point our education has often failed. The
process of translating the written language into
speech is so slow and difficult that a large share of
the pupils of our schools are condemned to compara-

tive ignorance. The words as they appear have no meaning to them. One who has acquired the power of directly receiving thought from the printed page, is endowed with a new intellectual faculty. His eye flashes along the pages of a book, and he comprehends whole sentences at a glance. It would not do to say that these rapid readers do not understand what they read. The fact is they understand much better than the slow reader. The mental power, being relieved from the necessity of translating, concentrates itself upon the thought, and the thought is understood and remembered. Our endeavor should be to give the pupils this power of eye reading from the first, so that they may continually profit by it and have no evil habits to overcome.

Oral Reading. When the habit of sight reading is acquired, oral reading will need but little attention. The oral expression is subordinate to correct eye reading, and its acquisition is largely incidental. When the pupil has power to take in the thoughts from the printed page directly, he will have but little difficulty in giving it proper oral expression in the language of the author. The pupil, being under the control of the thought obtained, must read the thought as naturally as he speaks.

In oral reading there are always two parties, the readers and the hearers. It is as important that pupils should be taught to obtain thoughts by listening as by reading; and to this end the other members of the class should close their books while one is reading, the test of the value of the exercise being their ability to reproduce the thoughts which they have heard.

Writing. While the pupil is acquiring this new use of the eye, and learning to read in the true significance of that term, he should be taught to write. This process is simply the production of the forms which represent thought, and which quicken thought in him. While silent reading is analogous to obtaining thought from the speech of others, it should be so presented to the pupil that he acquires it unconsciously while endeavoring to express his thought, and the exercise should be continued until the habit is formed of the hand responding as directly as the voice to the mind and to the mandates of the will.

First Principle. The first principle to be observed in teaching written language is, " that things are cognized as wholes." Language follows this law. Although it is taught by an indirect process, still, in its external characteristics, it follows the law of other objects.

The question arises, what is the whole? or what is the unit of expression? It is now quite generally conceded that we have no ideas not logically associ-

ated with others. In other words, *thoughts*, complete
in their relations, are the materials in the mind out of
which the complex relations are constructed.

It being admitted that the thought is the unit of
thinking, it necessarily follows that *the sentence is the*
unit of expression. One can assure himself of the
correctness of this view by watching the operations
of a little child, even before it is able to talk. You
may give such a child any direction which you ex-
pect will control its action, and leave out any part of
the sentence that is essential to its completeness, and
the child will not be influenced by it. It is true that
elliptical expressions are sometimes used, but the
missing portions are supplied in the mind, before action is produced. Let any one attempt to remember
a series of words so arranged as to express no complete thought, and he will see how absolutely we are
dependent upon the logical arrangement of language.
A speaker will have no difficulty in making himself
understood in any part of a large room, if he ad-
dresses the audience in connected and logical dis-
course. No one listening will be conscious of losing
a single word of what is said. But let the same
reader attempt to read the names of a dozen persons,
or give a list of disconnected words, and he will
hardly be able to pronounce them with sufficient dis-
tinctness to be understood, without repetition.

Second Principle. A second principle is, we acquire a knowledge of the *parts* of an object by first considering it as a whole. Repeated recognitions reveal the characteristics of the whole, so as to separate it from other things. We descend from the contemplation of the whole to the parts that compose the whole. Otherwise the parts would be more distinctly remembered than the whole. But this is contrary to experience. We have no difficulty in distinguishing one person from another, but if called upon to state exactly in what this difference consists we should be at a loss for a satisfactory reply, unless we have made the matter an object of special attention.

That words are no exception to this rule is obvious from the almost universal practice of writing out the word and looking at it as a *whole* to determine whether it is properly spelled. We have more confidence in our judgment of the appearance of a word as a whole, than in our ability to reproduce it in detail, notwithstanding this latter method is the one in which we have been drilled.

The sentence, when properly taught, will, in like manner, be understood as a whole, better than if presented in detail. The order indicated is, first the sentence, then the words, and then the letters. The sentence being first presented as a whole, the words are discovered, and after that the letters composing the words.

Third Principle. The third principle is that while language, oral or written, follows the laws of other objects so far as its material characteristics are concerned, it differs from other objects studied for their own sake, by being representative in its character. While it is to be recognized, it must be so recognized as to make the thought expressed by it the conscious object of attention.

In oral speech this is already the case. The written language is to be so acquired that the same results will follow. To do this, it must be taught by an *indirect* process. The language must be learned while the attention is directed to the thought it represents.

RECAPITULATION.

First.—Things are recognized as wholes.

Second.—Parts are recognized while contemplating the wholes.

Third.—The whole or unit in language is the sentence.

Fourth.—Words, as parts of a sentence, are discovered while recognizing the sentence.

Fifth.—Letters are discovered while contemplating words.

Sixth.—Language, especially written language, is

to be learned indirectly, while the attention is directed to the thought expressed.

Practical Hints. Before attempting reading, a child should be able to use language with considerable care and fluency. Few children attain this power before the age of six years. The child must also be made to feel at home in the school room and in the presence of his teacher. Without this freedom, the teacher can never judge correctly concerning the mental condition of the child. The timidity and self-consciousness of pupils when first entering school, cannot be overcome by direct teaching. The change of condition from home to school should be made as slight as possible, and the teacher should study to enter into the thoughts and feeling of the child. When sympathy is fully established between teacher and pupil, and the pupil feels as unrestrained as at home, the conditions for successful teaching are secured.

The class should be as devoid of formality and constraint as is consistent with the successful working of the school. Order for order's sake is not desirable. Requiring pupils to "toe the mark" or to assume any precise attitude distracts their attention from the lesson in hand, and tends to make machines of them and to deprive them of all spontaneity in action.

Children of ordinary health and intelligence are always active. To compel quiet for any considerable

time is to do violence to child nature. Neglecting
to provide for natural and necessary exercise is to
convert the school room into a prison house. The
mistake is often made of making education consist of
repression instead of development, and natural activities indispensible to achievements are ruthlessly sacri-
ficed to an ideal discipline, where quiet must be
maintained at all hazards.

Slates and pencils are acknowledged necessities,
and as the child acquires the use of his powers they
will be in constant requisition. Provision should also
be made for the unconstrained exercise of the pupils,
that will interest them and not disturb the school.
A vacant corner in the school room, or a platform
raised a few inches above the floor and supplied with
blocks for the children to play with would meet this
demand. Building blocks may be easily and cheaply
obtained by taking a common board dressed on both
sides, three-fourths of an inch thick, and sawing it
into strips one and one-half inches wide. These
strips should then be sawed into pieces three inches
long, giving to the blocks the relative proportion of
bricks. A few pieces should be left six inches long,
and a few of the common bricks sawed in two, to
give variety to the combinations made.

CHAPTER II.

EXERCISES BEFORE BOOKS ARE USED.

FIRST STEP.

The object of this step is to awaken thought in the mind of the child by means of objects, and to give to the thought complete oral expression.

The teacher should be provided with a number of objects such as may be readily handled. At first those only should be used that will admit of the use of the article *a* before the name.

With Objects in Hand. *First*—Let the teacher and each pupil take an object in hand.

The teacher will call upon one of the pupils to tell what he has, and in reply the pupil will probably hold up the object and pronounce its name.

Teacher—" Jane, what have you ? "

Jane—" A pencil."

Teacher—" Who has a pencil? "

Jane—" I have."

Teacher—" Now tell me all about it."

Jane—" I have got a pencil."

Teacher—"Very well? But will one of you tell me what he has, and leave out the word 'got'?"

Charles—"I have a knife."

Teacher—"That is right. Now Jane will try again. Tell me what you have."

Jane—"I have a pencil."

It is best to secure the proper expression from the children, though it may take some time. But if the teacher fails in this, she will hold up her own object, and say, "I have a book." Then call upon one of the children who will very likely respond properly, "I have a knife."

The form of expression once obtained, there will be very little difficulty in obtaining the similar expressions from each member of the class. Let each hold up his object and tell what he has. This done, let the children change objects, and repeat the exercise, telling what each one has.

Second—Next let two or three children take hold of the same object, and let one of them make the statement, "We have a doll."

At first, the children may be inclined to continue the old form of expression, and the teacher may be obliged to take hold of the object and make the proper statement, but the children will readily take the hint. Now, vary this form with the first, until

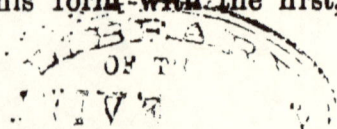

the children will instantly respond with the proper expression.

Third—Let one pupil hold an object and call upon another to make the statement. If a boy has the object, the response will be " He has a knife ; " if a girl, "She has a pencil."

Fourth—The teacher will hold an object, and the pupil will make the statement to the teacher, " You have a map."

Fifth—Two or more members of the class will hold an object, and one of the others will make the statement to the teacher, or .to the remaining members of the class, "They have a book."

These forms of expression will be repeated and changed in their order until there is no confusion or tendency to error in expression. The children should instantly respond with the appropriate expression.

Each teacher will select such subjects as the circumstances may require. The following list may serve as a hint to the kind of objects which may be used. When the object cannot be used, a toy or picture representing it may be substituted.

Book, slate, pencil, paper, knife, string, board, chalk, desk, seat, table, door, window, hat, cap, boot, shoe, clock, watch, doll, knife, match, wood, stove, girl, boy, man, woman, house, barn, dog, cat, cow, horse, rat, pig, sheep, glass, nail, etc.

In regard to words other than the names of familiar objects, the book which is to be used should be
taken as a guide.

With the Object in Sight. *First.* Place an
object before the class, and call upon a child to tell
what he sees, and he will respond, "I see a hat."

Let another speak for himself and his companions
with "We see a clock." Introduce the other pronouns with the verb *see*, as in the previous exercises.
Next introduce other verbs. A girl walks across the
floor, and the expression, "She walks," is elicited.
A boy will run, and the expression, "He runs," will
be obtained.

Second. Introduce the names of the different
members of the class, and use them in the place of
the pronouns in the previous exercises. Secure variety by using different verbs, as, "John sees the
clock," "Susan heard the watch tick," "James ran
home."

Third. Call attention to qualities of objects and
secure the appropriate expression, as, "John has a
large book," "Jennie has a white cat," "The black
dog barks."

The following list of qualifying adjectives is given
by way of suggestion.

Black, white, red, yellow, blue, green, brown,
large, small, little, big, good, bad, lazy, bright, tall,

short, hard, soft, rough, smooth, pleasant, light, heavy, dark, etc.

Fourth. Call attention to the position of object, and secure the proper expression, as, "The book is under the desk," "The bird flew over the tree." Continue this exercise until the more common prepositions have been used.

With one or more objects, expressions containing conjunctions and the plural form of the verb may be obtained, as, "A slate and a book are on the table," "John and Charles run," etc.

In general, any form of expression in common use may be obtained from the children by forming the proper concrete relations. These exercises constitute lessons in constructive language or composition, and should be continued until the children respond readily with the expression representing the exact relations of the things to which their attention is called.

This exercise may be varied by introducing object lessons with such simple descriptions as the children themselves may give. The children should also be encouraged to tell in complete sentences what they see out of school, on their way to and from school, and at home. They should give accounts of any interesting event which has happened to them, or which they may have observed. These exercises are especially valuable as preparing for the next step.

SECOND STEP.

The object of this step is to awaken in the mind of the child the exact thought contained in oral expression, and to lead him to make the appropriate concrete representation.

In observation we pass from the thought to the expression; in reading, from the expression to the thought. This step is to make clear that thought may be obtained from oral expression, as preparatory to the final step of obtaining thoughts from written expression.

The teacher will make a statement as "I have a knife," and will then ask, "What do I have?"

Pupil—"You have a knife."

Teacher—"How do you know that I have a knife?"

Pupil—"You said so."

The teacher will show the knife to confirm the statement.

The teacher will next call upon different members of the class to state what each has, confining the inquiries at first to objects at hand, and producing the object to confirm the statement.

Passing away from visible objects the children may be called upon to tell what they have at home. John may say "I have a large black dog," and Jane "I have a nice doll." The thoughts formed in the minds of the children are as vivid and as true as though verified by the production of the real object.

This step is a short one, and will require only a few exercises to accomplish its object.

THIRD STEP.

The object of this step is to awaken in the mind of the child the exact thought contained in written expression, and to enable him to express the thought in the language used. This is Reading.

While of necessity, in reading, the expression precedes the thought, no lesson will be a success where the expression fails to awaken the thought. The order in the third step is the same as in the second, with the substitution of written for oral expression.

The teacher goes to the board, and in a clear bold hand writes a sentence, as: "I have a knife." The pupils see the writing but of course do not know what it means. The teacher will call a pupil and put a knife into his hands, and the pupil in response to the impulse which is the result of previous training will instantly hold up the knife and say "I have a knife."

The teacher writes another sentence, as, "I have a pencil," and puts the object in the hands of another child who will respond, "I have a pencil."

The teacher will proceed in the same way until several children have objects in their hands, representing as many sentences upon the board.

The teacher will next call upon the first child to point out and read his sentence, which he will readily do as he still holds the object in his hand.

Each child, in turn, will be called upon to point out and read his particular sentence. When several are written upon the board, some child may forget which represents his statement, in which case the teacher will take the pointer and pass it over the sentence from left to right. The child will point out the sentence in the same manner, at the same time giving the oral expression. The pupil should not be allowed to guess, but when he hesitates, the teacher should point out the sentence for him.

Next, the pupils may exchange objects, and point out the sentence that expresses the new order of things under the same condition as before. It may be necessary frequently to erase sentences before the lesson is finished, but this will prove a help rather than a hindrance, as the pupil will more readily observe and remember the sentences by seeing them written.

These lessons are to be continued day after day, care being taken to vary the order and the objects, so that the children cannot recall the sentences by their location. The teacher's faith and patience may be severely tried, but steady progress is made. Each repetition strengthens and deepens the impression, until the association of the thought with its written representative is firmly made.

The objects used should be kept upon a table in sight and reach of the pupils. When a new sentence is written, the teacher may hand the object to the child, or point it out, allowing the pupil to take it himself. By varying the exercises in this manner, great activity may be secured on the part of the class.

A little further along the teacher may wait to give the pupils an opportunity to select the object without its being pointed out. When a child raises his hand and expresses a desire to do this, it shows that he has read the sentence, and is acting in obedience to the impulse occasioned by a comprehension of the thought. The oral reading follows as a natural consequence.

The trying point is now past. One after another will follow the example of the first, and read the sentences as they are written, independent of aid from the teacher. The child will indicate that he has read the sentence by raising his hand, and then, when permission is given, by selecting the proper object and "making it true," as the children express it, and by reading the sentence aloud with the object in hand.

An emulation will probably be excited, and each child will try to be the first to read. This may lead to guess-work on the part of the child, which the teacher will at once try to repress. The raising of the hand should be permitted only when the sentence has been read and the thought understood.

It is an easy matter to raise a false enthusiasm, indicated by raising the hand, snapping the fingers, rising from the seat, and various exclamations. These manifestations should be repressed, and that real enthusiasm stimulated which comes from certainty of results.

When a child reads a sentence from the board, he should indicate it by the pointer. At first the pupil will probably switch the pointer across the sentence and read it hurriedly at the same moment. These are symtoms of natural and healthful action, indicating that the thought is in the mind, and that the sentence is the unit of expression. The motion and utterance are simply in obedience to the impulse to speak the sentence as a unit. A little experience will serve to correct all that needs correction.

Variety in Expression. In using the first form of the sentence, as, " I have a book," and changing the object, the tendency on the part of the pupils will be to look only to the final word to determine the sentence. This should be corrected by changing the subject as well.

In the next changes, follow the order of the First Step, introducing cautiously the common pronouns, adjectives, verbs, prepositions and conjunctions. The names of the members of the class and the numerals up to ten should be early introduced. For suggestive lists, see explanation under First Steps.

Words are always used in their connections and made familiar by repetition in the expression of various shades of thought.

Analysis. Soon after children begin to read sentences, it will be found that they recognize individual words. From the study of a sentence as a whole they have discovered the elements or words of which the sentence is composed.

The use the child makes of the words at this time is peculiar. He evidently recognizes them, but has no impulse to pronounce them separately, or at all, until the sense is complete in his own mind. If, when the sentence is written, a strange word be present, he will make no effort to read any part of it. When the unknown word is explained and the sense thereby made complete he will read naturally and without hesitation.

This is a most healthful indication, and is a sure guide to the teacher in regard to the steps to be taken. It points out the exact difficulty which the child encounters, and enables the teacher to remove the difficulty with the greatest economy of time and energy. The introduction of new words is placed entirely within the control of the teacher, and the vocabulary of the pupil may be extended in any desirable direction. Care must be taken that the more active pupils do not monopolize the time, depriving the other members of the class of their share of the benefits.

As words become recognized as such, and their meaning understood from their office in the sentence, it may be well to write them upon a section of the board set apart for that purpose, so that the pupils may refer to them in their constructive work, and be sure of the correct forms. These lists are for reference and no other purpose.

Writing. Early in this step some, if not all, of the children will have the impulse to write. This should be encouraged. The first efforts will be directed to copying what they see written upon the board, but as the thought expressed is present in their minds they are in reality writing to express their thoughts. The first productions will of necessity be rude, but by a few judicious hints their muscles will be brought under proper control, principally through their own exertions.

The slates should be ruled to serve as a guide to the size of the letters. A few directions may be given in regard to holding the pen, the slant and size of letters, but not enough to distract the attention of the pupil from the thoughts he is endeavoring to express. In this way the children may attain great excellence in writing at an early period, and at the same time their penmanship will be as markedly individual as their faces.

Letters. While directing the writing the teacher will speak of the letters as though they were known to the pupils, showing the size of the m's, t's, l's, etc., and it will soon be discovered that the pupils can distinguish the letters and name them. This end has been accomplished without calling direct attention to them, and by the operation of the same mental laws that caused them to distinguish words.

Constructive Work. One of the most important educational ends is the ability to express thought clearly and fluently in writing. By the method here given the pupils early acquire this ability, and though the thoughts at first are simple, the mode of expressing them may be made perfect. Writing compositions is made as natural and easy as conversation, and the practice of reading compositions will make true intellectual reading more easy and certain.

Criticism. By this method, drill as it is common-
ly practised is entirely dispensed with. The thought
is the first object of attention, and if this be clear,
the expression will be natural and correct. Any ob-
scurity, either from the use of a new word, from the
construction of the sentence, or from not understanding the relations expressed, will manifest itself in the
inability of the child to read, or in his giving expression to a different thought.

The effort of the teacher in such cases must be directed to clearing up the thoughts. If the word is
new and the idea familiar, calling attention to the
idea will suggest the word or its equivalent. If the
idea and the word are both new, the teacher must
first develop the idea, creating in the mind of the
child the necessity for the word, and then give the
word. The custom of spending much time in "fish-
ing for words" from the child is an absurd one.
When the idea is fully developed, the word should
promptly be given, so that the two may be associated
together.

It is very easy to destroy the independence of the
pupils and substitute mechanical for intellectual reading, by the teacher's reading for the children to imi-
tate and by concert reading. Both should be avoided.

CHAPTER III.

READING FROM BOOKS.

In the exercises so far, the end in view has been to prepare the child to enter upon the work of reading from the printed page. If the work indicated has been well done, the pupil has acquired considerable power of thought and expression ; he has learned to regard the completed sentence as the expression of thought, and as having no significance unless the thought is understood ; he has learned to read readily what is written, and he has acquired a considerable skill in the expression of his own thoughts, by crayon and pencil. If this has been accomplished, he will have little difficulty in changing from written to printed matter.

Steps in Transition. Let the pupils look over some printed sentence made up of familiar words, and expressing a familiar thought, and if they experience any considerable difficulty in gaining the thought from the sentence, it will show that they are not ready for the change, and that written work should be continued.

When the time arrives for the transition, the teacher should select some easy lesson, and carefully examine it to find the words that the pupils will probably not know. These words are then to be made the basis of blackboard exercises in which their memory is developed, and they are used in the expression of thought by the pupils. In a familiar, conversational way, the teacher may excite an interest in the subject of the story, taking care not to tell the details so as to deprive the reading of the interest which comes from the new ideas obtained.

The books are put into the hands of the children after they are assembled in class. Let all the members of the class look at the first sentence, and when ready let each one raise his hand. Should a familiar word not be recognized in its printed form the teacher will write it on the board.

When all are ready the teacher will call upon one " to tell what the book says." The sentence will probably be correctly read. If mistakes are made in the reading, it will be because the pupil does not understand the sentence. Proceed in the same manner with each sentence to the end of the lesson.

If the class be large, the lesson may be read a second time by other members of the class, but care should be taken that the pupils do not learn the lesson by rote, and so repeat it without understanding.

Intelligence is the key to good work, and should be the sole guide to expression.

General Preparation. It will require but few lessons to make the transition from the board and slate exercises to the book. When this is made and the pupils are able readily to read the printed words, the regular work for preparing each reading lesson should be in the following order :

First—As in the transition exercises, the teacher will become familiar with the lesson beforehand, and will give the books to the children after they are arranged in class. This is to assure freshness of thought in the lesson read.

Second—The pupils will look over the lesson for unfamiliar words, and will indicate them to the teacher. As the object of the exercise is to gain the thought, new words must first become known.

Third—The pupils will then close their books, and the teacher will develop the meaning of each word by questions and familiar conversation.

Fourth—The pupils will use the new words in the construction of sentences, each one expressing a familiar thought. This kind of exercise has already become familiar to the pupils in their previous work.

Fifth—The new words, as their ideas are developed, will be written upon the board, so that the pupils may become familiar with their written forms.

As each word is written it will be seen that the pupils will carefully scrutinize it, as though it was an object of interest.

Sixth—Pupils look over each sentence carefully to see if they can understand the thought expressed. In case they do not, the teacher will develop and explain it.

Seventh—The pupil reads. As the words are all known and the thoughts understood before the pupil tries to read aloud, his reading will probably be ✓ natural and correct.

Penmanship. The writing, begun with the board exercises, will be continued after the books are introduced. The impulse to write comes from the desire to express thought to the eye, and skill in the use of the pencil or pen is acquired under this stimulus. With the mechanic, the impulse which controls his muscles and gives direction and force to his action, is the end to be accomplished. The knowledge of his tools is acquired indirectly and incidentally while using them. To withdraw his attention from the work and fix it upon the tools would be fatal to the work. So with the penmanship of the child. It should be acquired incidentally in the endeavor to express thought; and turning the direct attention from the thought to the writing, will be fatal to the highest success in writing. Intellectually, it would change a pleasing occupation into a mechanical and onerous task.

As the child learns the use of speech long before he learns the grammatical rules that govern speech, so he learns practically how to express his thoughts in writing long before he is in a condition to be benefited by the rules of penmanship. A few general hints may be given from time to time, as indicated in the Third Step, but the pupil's progress will depend upon the amount of practice which he has in the direction pointed out. By this practice, his muscles are brought gradually under control, imperfections are eliminated, and the habit of correct writing is formed.

Composition. The first lesson which the child received was in the formation and expression of thought, which was in reality oral composition. As soon as he acquires the ability to write legibly from copying the work from the board, he will begin to change his oral compositions into written ones. This constructive, written work will follow the same order, and accompany step by step the oral work already indicated. These first compositions furnish excellent reading lessons, for no two being alike one reads for the information of the others, conforming to the practice in real life.

Like all the other exercises in language, composition must not be taught directly, but success in it is attained incidentally in the endeavor to express thought. The ability of a child to use words correctly in oral or written composition is the only sure test of his understanding them. It requires far less familiarity with language to read mechanically, than it does to use the same language in the expression of our own thoughts.

Subject-Matter. The first lesson will be in connection with objects, as was given in the First Steps in reading. Next objects may be described. Then as new words are found, each one will be used in the expression of a thought and in the construction of a sentence.

The child may next be called upon to relate what has happened to him during the day, the incidents of a walk, or a play, or what he saw on his way to school. The teacher may tell a story or read something from a book, which the pupils will reproduce. The children may bring their own little books, and each one may read a story which the others will reproduce. In these latter exercises another important educational interest is served;—the pupils are taught to listen to what is said, and to repeat accurately what they heard.

Spelling. In this course no place is given to distinctive spelling lessons, as it is believed that such

lessons are productive of little else than mischief.
Nearly all the real study of the child involves
spelling as a necessary incident. If the forms of
words which he has always seen are correct, the
forms which he reproduces will also be correct. To
him a misspelled word is either no word at all, or an
unknown element to be learned like other new words.
The misspelled word is not recognized as expressing
the idea of the correctly spelled one. The child reads
with his eye, and while reading is not conscious of
the sounds of words. In the endeavor to express the
thought in writing, his hand responds to the impulse
which the thought gives, and in the way it was given.
As the thought was occasioned by form, speaking to
the eye, it will of necessity be reproduced in the
same form. Good spelling is the result.

Oral Elements. When oral spelling is practised,
a disturbing element is introduced. The attention is
partially diverted from the forms of the words to the
names of the letters that compose them, and language,
which should be used as a medium of thought, becomes the object of thought. The written and
printed page is deprived of its distinctive character of
being a direct representative of thought; the written
words must be translated into spoken words through
the medium of letters; and thus a direct barrier is
interposed between the mind of the child and the

thoughts contained in the lesson. This result is, of course, antagonistic to the eye and thought reading which is here advocated.

The phonic analysis of words should have no place 𝓏𝓛 in the primary schools. Until the habits of thought reading and correct spelling are well established, such analysis is a positive evil. It makes the child conscious of the oral element of words, and as these do not correspond with the written elements, a double evil ensues: the mind has become directly conscious of language which it should use unconsciously or nearly so; and it introduces a new set of elements antagonistic to the ones used in the graphic expression. The habitual action of the muscles coming from one stimulus, upon which good spelling depends, is directly interfered with by another stimulus which urges to different results. The antagonism is radical and irreconcilable, and bad spelling must result. The reason for the early introduction of the phonic element:—the securing of correct pronunciation, may be accomplished in another way. The pupils should be required to pronounce their words slowly, so as to give each sound its proper force, and here imitation of the words as spoken by others is the only way to secure correct results.

Correcting Mistakes. Under the system here advocated, mistakes in spelling, in punctuation, in the

use of capitals, etc., will be rare, but they will sometimes occur. The teacher's work should be as correct
as human vigilance can make it, and by this means
the pupil's mistakes will be reduced to a minimum.
The mistakes usually made in school are the result
of guess-work or of deliberate judgment, when language has become a subject of direct consciousness.
The mistakes made when this system is practised are
the results of some distracting element which has for
the moment disturbed habitual action. In the first
case the mistakes, being in the line of habitual action,
make a deep impression and tend to perpetuate themselves : in the second case, being opposed to habitual
action, they make but little impression and are easily
eradicated.

Upon noticing any error of this kind, the teacher
should at once erase it, and substitute the correct
form. The direct attention should be for the moment turned to this correct form, and the pupil
should write the word several times to make the
impression deeper. This is one of the rare instances
where the direct attention may be profitably diverted
from the thought to the expression. The sooner the
object is accomplished and the attention again turned
to the thought, the better for the pupil. The error
should never be brought into prominence, and if it

can be erased before the pupil has discovered it, all the better.

If a child is in doubt, he should indicate it, and the teacher should supply the correct form. The reason for this is obvious. The doubt has arrested habitual action, and made the word or phrase the object of direct attention. If left without assistance, the mind must exercise a judgment without the elements upon which a correct judgment can be based, and the chances are about even that a mistake will be made.

A mistake occuring under such circumstances will make a deep impression, and will tend still further to disturb habitual action, becoming the parent of numerous future mistakes. Constant practice under judicious direction is the only way to secure the highest and best results.

Reading Matter. A great difficulty is experienced in obtaining a sufficient supply of appropriate reading matter. The book given to any class should be within their comprehension, and it should be read through, or such parts of it as are found interesting. An ordinary first or second reader will last but a few weeks, and hence there should be in every school several such readers, or some equivalent reading matter.

By the exercise of judgment and tact, the teacher

may be able to secure several such readers for use, and as an important part of the reading exercise is for the pupils to learn to listen, it is not strictly necessary that each member of the class be supplied with the same book. A single copy of a book may be passed from hand to hand, and in this way not only may the text-books be utilized, but story-books which the children have at home may be used with profit. From this variety in reading, supplementing observation, the materials are gained for any amount of composition in the form of constructive and reproductive work.

In general, children should be induced to read what they desire to know, and what is worth knowing, and for the purpose of knowing. Hence, all through the course silent reading, followed by reproduction, should receive special attention. A story or sketch may be passed from child to child and read silently, and then reproduced in writing. Sometimes it may be reproduced orally, and indeed oral and written exercises should be constantly intermingled, so that children may become equally proficient in both forms of expression.

Economies. It will be seen that reading, writing, spelling, and composition are simultaneous operations by this method, and that all are subordinated to the thought gained and expressed. In this way much

time is gained, and the multitude of classes in un-
graded schools is diminished. These subjects are all
related to each other, and are dependent upon
thought; and to treat them separately is to destroy
this relation and dependence.

Again, by this method these subjects are all taught
incidentally. To teach them separately and directly
is to deprive written language of its legitimate function of being a direct representation of thought.

General Suggestions. Too much stress cannot
be laid upon the importance of careful and correct
work on the part of the teacher. Children at this
early age are confiding, and are ready to take what
the teacher has to give, "Bread or stones" are received with equal trustfulness. At the same time
they are easily confused, and ill-directed teaching ap-
pears in a slovenly recitation.

The teacher must not be anxious for immediate re- L
sults. Anxiety in this direction is a constant tempta-
tion to adopt those specious methods by which
apparent, rather than real progress is made. The
letter, word, or phonic method will each day accomplish certain specific results, which can be weighed
and measured. Teachers, parents and friends see
this, and are satisfied. But the results leave little
impress of true mental growth. Naming letters and
words, no matter in what order, and remembering

them, is not necessarily reading. The thought must be reached, and everything else must be subordinated to this end.

The child learns oral speech by degrees, adding word after word to his vocabulary, as its necessity is felt in expressing his own thought. Each new thought and new expression is assimilated by use. In reading and writing, the same law holds. New elements should be introduced no faster than they can be made familiar by use. The expression follows the thought. In this way the mind of the pupil grows by receiving its proper aliment, and the power of expression increases with each new acquisition of thought.

In this process time is an important element. An effort to cram defeats its own ends. Hurry retards. Crowding the memory with words weakens it for thought. Filling the mind with the forms of language that convey no thought, is like filling the stomach with husks,—no digestion follows. Worse than this, the mind overburdened with this crude material loses all power and inclination for real work.

The time necessary for each step cannot be precisely given, as it must vary with the capacity of the pupils, the tact of the teacher, and various conditions of the school. The pupils should not be advanced from the "first step" until they are able to give oral expression to any well defined thought without hesitation. The average time for this will be about one month. The "Second Step" will require but few lessons. Its objects should be accomplished in a week.

In the " First Step " the practice of allowing the children to construct the concrete relations, or, as they term it, " make true " the thought before reading it, should be continued several weeks. This exercise, more than any other, arouses activity, both physical and mental, and excites a permanent interest in the work. The average time for accomplishing all the work of the " Third Step " will be about two months, giving three months for the preliminary exercises before books are introduced.

When the children read a sentence that cannot be literally illustrated, they should feel that it is true in thought, and here comes in the exercise of the imagination. In the development and culture of this faculty, the teacher may find some difficulty. With their limited experience, children with active imaginations have not learned to distinguish between outward facts and thoughts which exist only in their own minds. This want of discrimination is often mistaken for moral delinquency. The remedy is found in the close observation of objects and facts and the literal descriptions which follow such obser-

vations. Making sentences " true " is one of these
corrective exercises.

A very common mistake should be carefully avoided, and that is the endeavor to fill the mind with the
matured and condensed results of scientific investigation. True education is a growth. The knowledge
upon which the mind feels must be assimilated.
This knowledge must be administered in such pro-
portions and under such conditions as will best
promote assimilation. The effort to cram ideas is
as fatal as that of cramming words. The reasoning processes of maturity do not belong to child-
hood. The true education does not deal so much
in the results of scientific discovery as in its
methods. These methods are: first, the observation
of objects, by which facts are obtained, and the ob-
serving powers cultivated; second, the expression of
these facts in oral and written language, by which
process the facts become clearly defined and perma-
nently retained; third, the observation of relations,
by which comparisons and generalizations are made,
and general principles reached; and fourth, the application of these principles, by which the more
subtle relations are discovered and the reasoning
powers are fully developed. To reverse this process
and commence with the reasoning, would be equivalent to laying upon the 'shoulders of children the bur-

dens of mature manhood. No matter with how much care this may be done, or what may be the apparent immediate results, the permanent result is distortion and deformity.

www.ingramcontent.com/pod-product-compliance
Lightning Source LLC
Chambersburg PA
CBHW031808090426
42739CB00008B/1221